Going Places

ON A BOAT

By Robert M. Hamilton

Gareth Stevens
Publishing

Please visit our website, www.garethstevens.com. For a free color catalog of all our high-quality books, call toll free 1-800-542-2595 or fax 1-877-542-2596.

Library of Congress Cataloging-in-Publication Data

Hamilton, Robert M., 1987-
Going places : on a boat / Robert M. Hamilton.
    p. cm.
Includes index.
ISBN 978-1-4339-6271-4 (pbk.)
ISBN 978-1-4339-6272-1 (6-pack)
ISBN 978-1-4339-6269-1 (library binding)
1. Boats and boating—Juvenile literature. I. Title.
VM150.H263 2012
623.82—dc23

                                    2011030081

First Edition

Published in 2012 by
Gareth Stevens Publishing
111 East 14th Street, Suite 349
New York, NY 10003

Copyright © 2012 Gareth Stevens Publishing

Editor: Katie Kawa
Designer: Andrea Davison-Bartolotta

Photo credits: Cover, pp. 1, 5, 9, 11, 13, 15, 17, 19, 21, 23, 24 (all) Shutterstock.com; p. 7 (left) Jupiterimages/Creatas/Thinkstock; p. 7 (right) 3777190317/Shutterstock.com.

Printed in the United States of America

CPSIA compliance information: Batch #CW12GS: For further information contact Gareth Stevens, New York, New York at 1-800-542-2595.

Contents

Boats move on water.

Some boats are slow.
Some are very fast!

The front of a boat
is called the bow.

The back of a boat
is called the stern.

Some boats have sails.
These boats need wind
to move.

Some sails are squares.
Some are triangles.

15

Some boats need oars.
An oar is a kind
of pole.

People push the oars
in the water.
They row the boat.

People use boats
to catch fish.

A ship is a big boat. Many people can fit on a ship.

Words to Know

oars

sails

Index